多元的家庭

Social Emotional and Multicultural Learning | Non-Fiction Series

Copyright © 2022 by Level Learning, INC. and Washington Yu Ying PCS™
Original and Edited Text Copyright © 2022 by Washington Yu Ying PCS™

All rights reserved. No part of this book in whole or part may be reproduced without written permission from the publisher.

Published by Level Learning, INC.

Content Contributors:
Washington Yu Ying PCS™
Level Learning - Ya-Ching Chang

Illustrations by: Josh Taira

Leveling classification based on Level Learning standard. For full description, visit www.levellearning.com

ISBN 978-1-64040-087-0
Simplified Chinese Edition

About Level Learning:

Level Learning provides a literacy focused curriculum specifically designed for K-12 Chinese as a Second Language classrooms. Our program offers 20 levels of specific and detailed objectives, leveled texts and passages, mastery-based online assessment, and analytics to enable data-driven instruction. Level Learning reading curriculum for both literature and informational text emphasize grammar and comprehension skills to help teachers develop confident and independent Chinese language readers. The non-fiction series of books are specifically designed to support our informational text course based on multiple national standards. To learn more about our entire offering, visit www.levellearning.com.

About Washington Yu Ying PCS™:

Washington Yu Ying PCS is a Mandarin English dual language immersion International Baccalaureate (IB) World school. Yu Ying's mission is to inspire and prepare young people to create a better world by challenging them to reach their full potential in a nurturing Chinese/English educational environment. Yu Ying's comprehensive IB, dual immersion curriculum equips students with global competencies for success in the real world. As a leader in immersion education, Yu Ying is determined to advance Chinese language programs and global citizenry education by helping other schools create and strengthen their Chinese programs. For more information, email: products@washingtonyuying.org

大部分的家庭都是由爸爸妈妈和孩子组成的。在一个家庭中,丈夫和妻子有着不同的责任。丈夫外出工作,妻子则在家做家务和照顾孩子。

但是，随着时代的发展和人们思想的进步，家庭分工发生了变化。有些家庭，丈夫和妻子都外出工作；有些家庭则是妻子出去工作，丈夫在家做家务和照顾孩子。丈夫和妻子的责任不再因为性别而不同。

另外,现代的家庭结构也开始变得多元化,除了一夫一妻以外,还出现了同性家庭和单亲家庭。

"同性家庭"就是由两个男性或两个女性组成的家庭。在早期,同性家庭是不被接受的,同性恋者也因此受到了许多不平等的对待。

2015年6月26日，美国最高法院通过了全美同性恋者可以结婚的法案。渐渐地，人们开始接受有两个爸爸或两个妈妈的家庭结构。

"单亲家庭"指家庭中除了孩子外只有一个父亲或一个母亲所组成的家庭。造成单亲家庭的原因很多,比如因为父母分开,孩子只能跟着其中一人生活,又比如未婚生子或父母其中一人死亡等。

因为没人一起分担责任，一般来说，单亲家庭的生活也会比其他家庭更辛苦。

另外，有的父母分开了，又和别人组成新的家庭。生活在这种的家庭的孩子，需要花较多的时间去接受生活上的改变。

这些生活上的改变,包括离开原来的家,学习适应新的家庭、新的家人和不同的生活方式等。

除此之外，有的家庭会选择收养儿童。这些被收养的孩子可能来自美国，也可能来自其他国家。有的家庭也会收养身体上有残疾的孩子，给这些孩子更好的关爱和生活。

美国是一个多元的社会，了解不同的家庭结构，可以让我们更容易接受来自不同环境的人。

Glossary

	Pinyin	English Definition
组成	zǔ chéng	to form
丈夫	zhàng fu	husband
妻子	qī zi	wife
责任	zé rèn	responsibility
家务	jiā wù	housework
照顾	zhào gù	to take care of
发展	fā zhǎn	development
思想	sī xiǎng	thinking
性别	xìng bié	gender
结构	jié gòu	structure
多元化	duō yuán huà	diversification, many kinds
同性	tóng xìng	same sex
单亲	dān qīn	single parent
平等	píng děng	equality
对待	duì dài	treatment

	Pinyin	English Definition
最高法院	zuì gāo fǎ yuàn	Supreme Court
结婚	jié hūn	marriage
法案	fǎ àn	law
接受	jiē shòu	to accept, to receive
原因	yuán yīn	reason
未婚	wèi hūn	unmarried
死亡	sǐ wáng	to die, death
分担	fēn dān	to share
适应	shì yìng	to adapt
生活方式	shēng huó fāng shì	way of life
选择	xuǎn zé	to choose
收养	shōu yǎng	to adopt
残疾	cán jí	disablity
环境	huán jìng	situation

www.ingramcontent.com/pod-product-compliance
Lightning Source LLC
Chambersburg PA
CBHW041220070526
44584CB00001B/35